FIERCE  CREATURES

by Helen Orme

Copyright © **ticktock Entertainment Ltd 2003**
First published in Great Britain in 2003 by ticktock Media Ltd.,
Unit 2, Orchard Business Centre, North Farm Road, Tunbridge Wells, Kent, TN2 3XF.

We would like to thank:
David Gillingwater, Duncan Bolton at Bristol Zoo and Elizabeth Wiggans.
Illustrations by Simon Clare Creative Workshop.

Picture Credits:
Alamy images: 7, 16-17, 18-19, 26-27, 28. Corbis: OFC, 1, 4-5, 8-9, 10-11, 12-13, 20-21, 22-23, 24-25, 29, 30-31, OBC. Natural Science Photos: 14-15 (Bob Cranston).

Every effort has been made to trace the copyright holders, and we apologize in advance for any unintentional omissions. We would be pleased to insert the appropriate acknowledgements in any subsequent edition of this publication.

ISBN 1 86007 348 4 pbk
ISBN 1 86007 338 7 hbk
Printed in Hong Kong

Contents

All words appearing in the text in bold, **like this**, are explained in the glossary.

Think...

What special hunting skills do fierce creatures have?

Which animals do they eat?

Do they hunt alone or in groups?

Almost all creatures we think of as fierce are **carnivores**, or meat eaters. These creatures use different hunting skills to catch their food. Once they catch their **prey**, they use their teeth or sharp claws to kill it!

Imagine...

How would you feel if you were an animal's prey?

It looks as though you are about to find out...

Oh, no! I'm being followed!

This is a grizzly bear.

The grizzly bear is the fiercest **mammal** in North America. Female bears can be especially dangerous when they are protecting their cubs! Grizzlies can run as fast as 30 miles per hour (mph). Even horses have difficulty escaping from a rushing grizzly.

Grizzly Bears are **omnivores** (they eat plants and other animals).

Their coats are usually dark brown.

Look at these huge teeth!

Grizzlies are experts at catching salmon.

They have big, powerful jaws and sharp claws, which can be as long as a human finger.

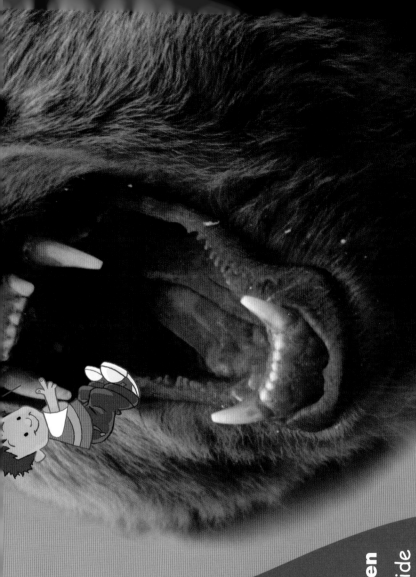

Grizzlies eat a lot of food during the summer to build up their body fat. This helps them stay alive through their long winter hibernation.

Do not disturb until spring!

Grizzly bears **hibernate** for up to half the year. They build a **den** on the north side of a hill, where the snow stays frozen all winter long. The snow helps to keep the den warm.

Lions live in groups called *prides*. A pride usually has about 15 lions, and most of them will be related. Each pride has its own **territory**.

The thick mane around a lion's neck protects it when it fi

Male lions mark their territories with **scent**. They also roar to scare away other males.

Roar!

Lions often hunt at night.

A lion's roar can be heard almost five miles away.

This is a lion.

Lions live in Africa on grassy **plains** and in open woodlands. They work in teams to **stalk** and then **ambush** their prey. Lions eat wildebeests, impalas, zebras, buffaloes, and wild hogs. Sometimes they even steal the prey that other animals have killed!

A female lion is called a lioness. It does not have a mane around its neck.

Although male lions are bigger than females, the female lions do most of the hunting!

Can you spot what this is?

It's a cheetah.

Cheetahs are the world's fastest land animals.
They hunt gazelles, impalas, wildebeests,
and other fast-running animals.
If the cheetah wants to survive,
it has to be faster than
the animals it hunts.

Top sprinter!

Cheetahs have yellow-gray fur with dark spots.

Cheetahs can run as fast
as 70 mph. This is as fast
as a car on a freeway!

But cheetahs cannot run fast for very
long. If they do not catch their
prey quickly, they have to rest
before they can try again.

Cheetahs have thinner bodies and longer legs than most members of the cat family.

Cheetahs have weak jaws and small teeth. If they see a large **predator** like a lion, they run away to protect themselves!

A cheetah's fur makes it difficult for other animals to see it in tall grass. This **camouflage** helps protect it.

Male killer whales have the tallest dorsal fins of any animal. Their dorsal fins can grow up to six feet high, or as tall as a man.

The dorsal fin helps a killer whale with high-speed swimming.

Killer whales live in family groups called pods. A pod can have between 5 and 30 members.

Killer whales "talk" to each other with a mixture of whistles, screams, and clicks. Each pod has a slightly different language.

This is an orca.

The blowhole is here.

The killer whale, or orca, is really a type of dolphin. It is the biggest member of the dolphin family. Killer whales have powerful, stocky bodies and lots of teeth!

whooshhh!

Killer whales eat seabirds, turtles, fish, squid, seals, sea lions, and even other dolphins or whales! They eat any creature that swims or floats!

Whales breathe through their blowholes. When killer whales come to the surface, they blow ten feet high fountains of air and water out of their blowholes. This helps to clear them.

15

No! It's a great white shark.

Great white sharks eat fish, sea lions, seals, turtles, small whales, and even other sharks! They also eat any dead animals that they find floating in the water.

Great white sharks have around 3,000 teeth, which are in rows.

A shark's most important sense is smell. It can sense just one drop of blood in 26 gallons of water!

Sharks have a full mouth of teeth!
If a tooth is broken off or lost, it is
replaced by a tooth from the next row.

Sharks have a gray coloring on their backs. This makes it difficult for them to be seen when they attack animals from underneath.

Each tooth is up to three inches long.

Sharks are heavier than the water they swim in.
If they stop moving, they will sink. Great whites
move through the water by using their powerful
tails. Their fins are only used for balance.

Scientists think that wolves can "talk" to each other by making different faces. When wolves show their teeth and point their ears forward, they are posing a threat.

Wolves have two layers of fur to keep them warm.

Wolves take good care of their young. The males hunt for food and then bring it back to the **den**. As the wolf cubs grow, the mother and other members of the pack help to feed them.

This is a wolf.

Wolves live and hunt in groups called *packs*. They have their own territories, but they sometimes travel far away from them to hunt. When the pack is together, it often howls loudly. This keeps the wolves alert, ready to hunt, and in contact with one another.

Wolves hunt and kill prey up to ten times heavier than their own weight.

They have long fur on the outside layer and short fur next to the skin.

Howl!

Howling is like a wolf telephone! The sound travels long distances.

The hippo's ears, nose, and eyes are on the top of its head. It can stay mostly underwater and still watch what is going on around it.

A hippo's ears and nostrils can be closed so that water can't get in.

Hippos are **herbivores**, or plant eaters, who spend most of the day resting in water. They can stay underwater for up to 30 minutes.

This is a hippopotamus.

Hippos can be fierce fighters.

Hippos might appear quiet and peaceful, but if something alarms them, they can become some of the most dangerous animals in Africa!

Males have huge teeth, which can grow to more than two feet long.

When a hippo opens its mouth wide, it may be trying to scare other hippos away.

A hippo can bite a crocodile in half and can reach a top speed of 19 mph when it runs.

This is a golden eagle.

Golden eagles hunt small land animals, such as rabbits. They also hunt other birds such as seagulls, crows, and owls. Sometimes they feed on **carrion** and may even kill large animals that are weak or sick.

Golden eagles build some of the world's largest nests.

The golden eagle sometimes catches large birds, such as geese and cranes, in mid-air.

It gets its name from the golden-colored feathers on its neck.

The adult eagle's body is usually dark brown.

Golden eagles can carry up to six pounds

If food is scarce golden eagle chicks will often kill and eat their younger brothers and sisters.

Adult birds have a wingspan of six to seven feet.

Golden eagles build their nests in tall trees or on high, jagged rocks. Sometimes these places have been used for many years by many families of eagles.

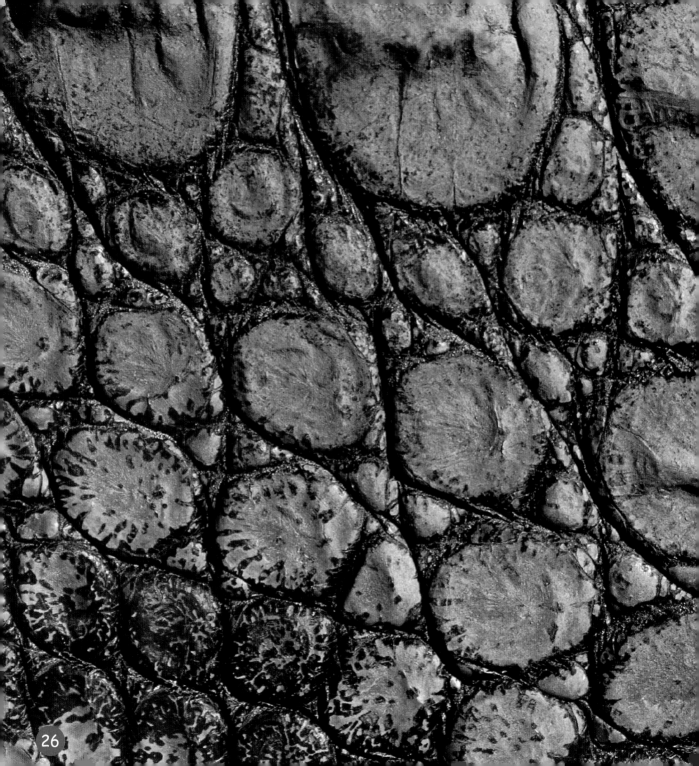

Is this some dried mud?

A crocodile waits for its prey to come down to the water's edge for a drink.

Crocodiles can catch large animals, such as young hippos, buffaloes, giraffes, and even lions!

The crocodile slowly swims to the shore. It lies in wait, with just its eyes above the water. Then, it lunges out of the water and grabs its victim's head, pulling the animal into deeper water to drown it.

Hide me!

A crocodile has powerful jaws that can crush the bones of its prey.

No! It's a crocodile.

Crocodiles are **reptiles**. They are cold-blooded and must lie in the sun to warm up their bodies.

Tough skin protects the crocodile against rock damage and enemy attacks!

To keep safe, baby crocodiles hide inside their mothers' mouths.

Crocodiles can see with their eyes closed! They have an extra see-through eyelid that protects their eyes underwater.

GLOSSARY

AMBUSH To attack from a hidden position.

CAMOUFLAGE An animal's colorings or markings that match its surroundings and help to keep it hidden.

CARNIVORES Plants or animals that feed on other animals.

CARRION The meat from an animal that has already died.

DEN An animal's home or sleeping place.

HERBIVORES Animals that eat only plants.

HIBERNATE To sleep through the winter.

MAMMAL An animal with warm blood that produces milk for its young.

OMNIVORES Animals that eat both meat and plants.

PLAINS Flat areas of land.

PREDATOR An animal that lives by hunting, killing, and eating other animals.

PREY An animal that is hunted for food by another animal.

REPTILES Cold-blooded animals with scaly skins.

SCENT A special smell left by an animal.

SENSE Most people and animals have five senses: sight, smell, hearing, touch, and taste.

STALK To follow something without being seen.

TERRITORY The area that one animal protects and defends against other animals to keep its food supply and family safe.

INDEX